Discovering
YOUR
DESTINY

Discovering
YOUR
DESTINY

Bob Gass

Bridge-Logos
Alachua, FL 32615, USA

Bridge-Logos

Alachua, FL 32615, USA

Discovering Your Destiny

Library of Congress Catalog Card Number: 20-01089642

International Standard Book Number: 978-0-88270-863-8

Bible translations (abbreviations) used:
NIV   New International Version, Copyright © 1973,1978,1984 by the International Bible Society. Used by permission of Zondervan Bible Publishers.
TLB   The Living Bible, Copyright © 1971 by Tyndale House Publishers, Wheaton, IL. Used by permission.
TM   The Message, Copyright © by Eugene H. Peterson, 1993,1994,1995. Used by permission of NavPress Publishing Group
NAS   New American Standard, Copyright © 1960, 1962, 1963, 1968, 1971, 1972, 1973, 1975, 1977 by the Lockman Foundation Used by permission.
KJV   King James Version
CEV   Contemporary English Version, Copyright © 1995 by Thomas Nelson. Used by permission.
AMP   Amplified Bible, OT Copyright © 1965, 1987 by The Zondervan Corporation. The Amplified NT copyright © 1954, 1958, 1987 by the Lockman Foundation. Used by permission.
NLT   New Living Translation , Copyright © 1999 by Tyndale House Publishers. Used by permission.

Dedication

To Vivian and Barbara, in His goodness
God found you and brought us all together again,
after 50 years apart. And I'm thrilled about it.

also

To my wife Debby, who gladly goes
the second mile, and as many more as it takes
to get the job done.

also

To my wee sister Ruth, who spent many hours
editing, correcting, and improving
her big brother's writing.

Table of Contents

Preface

"Now choose life so that you and your children may live" (Deuteronomy 30:19 NIV).

Author Danny Cox writes, "I currently possess everything I've truly wanted and deserve. If I'm unhappy with what I have received, it's because I have not yet paid the required price. I've lingered too long at the quibbling stage.

"I am the sum total of the choices I have made and continue to make daily. What I now put under close scrutiny is the value of each upcoming choice. Therein lies the quality of my life-style. Will my future belong to the old me, or the new me? The answer to that depends on my attitude toward personal growth.

"The time left is what counts, and I am personally responsible for how that time is filled. With newfound maturity, I accept total responsibility for how good I can become at what is most important to me.

"With personal growth comes fear of the unknown

and new problems. These problems, however, are nothing more than the lengthening shadow of my personal growth. So I now turn my very real fear, with God's help, into a very real adventure. My life now expands to meet my newfound destiny. Old me, meet the new me!"

This book is the third in a series on living successfully. In the first book I dealt with Forgetting Your Past. In the second, I addressed Starting Over. In this one, I'd like to help you Discover Your Destiny.

I pray that these principles, some of which I'm still learning, will give you direction, and cause you to "choose life."

If you're ready for the journey—let's go!

Chapter One

Get Over Your Past!

We each have a past. It's either our prison, our excuse, or our springboard to the future. One thing is certain, until we break the chain that ties us to it, we can never move forward.

Recently, I saw a big Irish wolfhound chained to a post in a neighbor's back yard. And the chain was all the more cruel because of the dog's obvious desire to be free. Haven't you seen the same thing? People who should have been movers and shakers reduced to wimps and whiners. Why? Because they're chained to the past by an unforgiving heart.

Just a single chain around the big dog's neck incapacitated its entire body. That's how it works! Bitterness is like a chain around the neck of your potential; choking the life out of your freedom and joy, and making even the sweet taste of success turn sour in your mouth.

Maybe you've been hurt, and you're saying, "I'll never forgive them unless they admit what they've done, and ask for my forgiveness." What if they never do? Why should your happiness depend on their ability to do what's right—especially if they're not in the habit of doing it? You're giving them too much power!

Jesus said, "The thief cometh ... to steal, and to kill, and to destroy" (John 10:10). Note: he's a thief! Unforgiveness is the window through which he enters, and you are the only one who can close it! When you wake up and realize how much he's already stolen from you, you'll be angry with yourself.

When Jesus was on the Cross, He defeated His enemies by refusing to hold a grudge. He prayed, "Father, forgive them; for they know not what they do" (Luke 23:34). Once He said those words, He moved to a different realm—and you can too!

My grandson once had a toy car. He could move it anywhere at will, because there was a mechanism inside it that responded to a remote control in his hand. He just pushed the button, and off it went.

However, if I disconnected the mechanism in the car, he could push the button until he was blue in the face, and nothing happened.

That's how unforgiveness works. It can be triggered by a telephone call, a face in the crowd, a song, a particular date, or just a casual comment. What a miserable way to live!

You ask, "What's the solution?" Remove the mechanism that triggers the old feelings! How? By forgiving! Paul says, "Forgive one another as quickly and thoroughly as God ... forgave you" (Ephesians 4:32 TM).

The word forgive literally means "to get it out." It has nothing to do with the other person. It's a decision you make; like expelling carbon dioxide from your body, because you know that holding on to it will only hurt you. Release it. Go ahead—exhale! Let all that bitterness and unforgiveness out, and breathe in God's love.

The test of love is to forgive the guilty. That's what God did for you, and that's what He commands you to do for those who've hurt you. Can you pass that test? Or are you refusing to forgive them for things that aren't any worse than some of the stuff you've done? Forgive them, or you'll never be free to enjoy the relationship God wants you to have with them.

Are you struggling with a parent who abandoned or abused you? Forgive and release them; otherwise you'll waste all your emotional energy keeping them in the prison of your resentment. Think what that does to you!

Whatever you don't forgive you're destined to repeat. When you harbor resentment, it causes you to keep striking out at others, and in the process, robs you of the joy of loving and being loved in return. What a loss!

Unforgiveness is the umbilical cord that keeps you tied to the past. When you forgive, you cut that cord. When you refuse to, you remain tethered to memories that can affect you for the rest of your life. That's how issues pass from generation to generation. Take charge today by saying, "This ends here and now, and it ends with me!"

Learn to receive forgiveness from God—and from those you have hurt. Then offer it to those who have hurt you. When you can do that, your heart will be tender, your spirit will be light, your mind will be free, your vision will be clear, and your speech will be filled with kindness.

Life's too short to be an inmate in the prison of

past mistakes. Have you heard of that prison? Its jailers are guilt and regret, and if you let them, they'll hold you captive, torturing you with images of what could have been or should have been if only you'd done this or that.

Decide today to live by the three "R's." Repent, Rectify the situation if possible, and take Responsibility for your life. Once you've done that, close the book, enjoy the benefits of God's grace, and move beyond guilt.

Recognize when something is dead. No amount of work will resuscitate a corpse, so sign the death certificate, bury the past, and move on. That doesn't mean you're quitting—it just means you're conserving your strength for the things that count, and about which you can do something.

Peter writes, "Casting all your care upon Him; for He careth for you" (1 Peter 5:7). The Greek interpretation of the word cast means, "throw it away!" What are you dragging around from your past—old pain, old scars, or a torch for somebody who's already moved on? God's Word to you today is—"Throw it away!" You're sacrificing your future to an idol that's not worthy of your worship.

Why would God tell you to do something so

radical? Because "He careth for you." That's right; while you're caring for it, He's caring for you. It's hard to watch somebody you love twisting in pain because of something they shouldn't be carrying to begin with.

God has no problem making the thing leave you alone. His struggle is in getting you to loosen your grip on it! So He speaks to you—not what's bothering you—and says, "Throw it away!"

You say, "But I've made so many mistakes." The heroes of the Bible were powerful, but they weren't perfect. They were chastised, but they were never discarded! And their human frailty should encourage you to believe that you can be used by God too.

Actually the contrast between the people God uses and the God who uses them reminds us who is to be worshipped.

Paul readily admitted that he fell far short of his goal, yet the light that shone from his earthen vessel still illuminates our walk 2,000 years later. A perfect word from imperfect hands—that's "the high calling of God," and it's through ordinary people like you and me that He chooses to fulfill it. Amazing!

In Hebrews, chapter eleven, notice what God says concerning some of His heroes: "Out of weakness were made strong ..." (Hebrews 11:34). They were strengthened through struggle. Don't judge them by a weak moment judge them by the entirety of their lives. The dent in their armor didn't affect their performance on the battlefield. They're not remembered because they were flawless; they're remembered because of their faith.

"Why does God use people like that?" you ask. Because: (a) His strength is made perfect in our weakness (2 Corinthians 12:9). (b) He's not limited by our limitations (Ephesians 3:20). (c) He uses what's available (1 Corinthians 1:27). Aren't you glad?

Jesus said, "The stone which the builders rejected ... is become the head of the corner: this is the Lord's doing, and it is marvelous in our eyes" (Matthew 21:42).

Jesus concluded that the rejection of men was "the Lord's doing." Joseph did too. After he'd been betrayed by his family, he said, "Ye thought evil against me; but God meant it unto good" (Genesis 50:20). Can you say that too? Instead of obsessing over what somebody else is doing to you, can you see what God is doing for you? He orchestrates what the enemy does, and makes it accomplish His purposes in your life. Marvelous!

How often have you gone through something

and later realized that it was necessary? If you hadn't sustained this or walked through that, you wouldn't be ready for the blessing you're enjoying now. Right?

It's when you begin to see God in it that it becomes "marvelous" in your eyes. When that happens, you can stand up and say, "Here's how I see it. It took all I've been through to make me what I am today. Therefore, I choose to be better, not bitter. I trust the faithfulness of God. If He doesn't move this mountain, He'll give me strength to endure until tomorrow. And if it's not gone by tomorrow, I'll still believe He's able, and trust Him until He does."

People will enter your life and people will leave it, but God's promise to you is "You will be blessed when you come in and blessed when you go out" (Deuteronomy 28:6 NIV). Rejection can actually bring divine direction, and become "marvelous" in your eyes when you start to see the hand of God in it all.

Chapter Two

Build Your Self-Worth

Before you can discover what God has called you to do, or reach your full potential, you've got to find a lasting basis on which to build your self-worth.

By the time you reached twelve, you'd already lived 4,380 days, and been molded by the words you'd heard—and in some cases, the ones you should have heard, and didn't.

Dorothy Law Nolte writes:

If a child lives with criticism, he learns to condemn,

If a child lives with hostility, he learns to fight,

If a child lives with ridicule, he learns to be shy,

If a child lives with shame, he learns to feel guilty,

If a child lives with tolerance, he learns to be patient,

If a child lives with encouragement, he learns to be confident,

If a child lives with praise, he learns to appreciate,

If a child lives with fairness, he learns justice,

If a child lives with security, he learns to have faith,

If a child lives with approval, he learns to like himself,

If a child lives with acceptance and friendship,

He learns to find love in the world.

Have you heard about the mother of the three preschoolers, who was asked if she'd still have children if she had to do it over again? "Sure," she responded. "Just not the same three!"

You smile, but many of us grew up with words that made us feel unimportant, unqualified, and unwanted. Those were the words that formed our shadow-beliefs.

Wherever you are today, look at your beliefs—they got you there!

Oprah Winfrey says, "When I was growing up in Mississippi, I never believed what people said about being poor, or black, or female. I believed I was God's child, therefore I could do anything. One day, when I was four, I watched my grandmother hanging clothes on a line. She said, 'Pay attention girl, you're going to have to do this someday too.' Inside I said, 'No, I won't.'

"In kindergarten I told my teacher, 'I don't belong here because I can read, and I know big words like elephant and hippopotamus.' The next day I was promoted to first grade.

"What I couldn't articulate then, but knew deep inside, was that I could do better—and that knowledge has been a constant in my life."

Just as your beliefs can move you forward, your shadow-beliefs can hold you back. You say, "What are shadow-beliefs?" The committee in your head that tells you you're not able, not worthy, or that you'll never make it.

What are your shadow-beliefs? Today I challenge you to bring them out into the light and expose them to God's Word. Don't let them control you, or decide your future. Refuse to translate any thought into a word if it contradicts what God says about you. You can't speak death over your dreams, and expect to see them come to life.

Paul says, "He hath chosen us ... before the foundation of the world" (Ephesians 1:4). Even if nobody valued you or showed you love in any way, this verse shatters and dispels all rejection by letting you know that God chose you. Imagine—called by God to be His child—hand-crafted for a specific purpose—chosen to be part of His body on earth—at precisely this time—and in precisely this location! Wow!

You weren't just some piece of wood that fell through a crack, and God said, "Oh, all right, let's go ahead and add it to the house." No! You came pre-cut to fit a particular place that nobody else except you could fill. You were selected just like the cedars of Lebanon—one-by-one—for the building of a temple (1 Corinthians 6:19).

So stop trying to be like somebody else! If you give up being who you are in order to become like them, you'll end up being somebody God doesn't need one more of. He made you in a precise way for a precise purpose, and only you will do. Think— regardless of what you like or dislike about yourself, you must be okay, because God chose you!

But you say, "Others don't seem to think much of me." So what? The Bible says, "The Lord knoweth them that are His" (2 Timothy 2:19). The prophet Samuel may have wanted to pick one of Jesse's other sons to be king, but he couldn't—because God had already chosen David!

Stop doubting yourself or competing with others. Nobody can take what God has reserved for you!

Farai Chideya graduated from Harvard, worked for Newsweek, and rose to the top of her profession. Yet she spent years living in the private hell of bulimia, trying to become like the glossy images in the make-believe world around her.

When she finally broke free from the destructive grip of her disease, she wrote, "Losing weight didn't change my personality, and it didn't lighten the emotional baggage I carried from my childhood. I thought I wanted to be thin. What I really wanted was to be happy, and neither my looks nor my achievements could do that. Because I couldn't love or accept myself, the acceptance of others was never enough. When I tried to be perfect, I came across as remote and unapproachable, the exact opposite was what I wanted."

Then she shares four life-changing principles. She says, "Your obsession to be perfect will: (1) keep you trapped in loneliness, for satisfying relationships can only be built on honesty and openness; (2) force you to see your shortcomings as something to hide, instead of opportunities for growth; (3) keep you fixated on what you're going to be someday, instead of enjoying what you are right now—present tense; and (4) rob you of the chance to make your life count, for by focusing constantly on yourself, you'll have nothing left to give to others." What insight!

Today, you have a choice: either others determine your worth or God does. Now, since you don't have to earn His love, and you're in no danger of losing it, that choice seems pretty clear, doesn't it?

In Genesis 1:31 we read, "God saw everything that he had made, and indeed, it was very good" (NRS).

Before you were born—God saw you. He knew the specific purpose you were designed to fulfill, so He provided you with the gifts you'd need, and the environment required to put it all together. Then He looked at you and said, "Very good!"

Can you say that too? It's important that you can, because others will only treat you according to how you treat yourself. If you don't like the way people respond to you, stop and ask yourself, "What's the message I'm sending?" In order to be treated well, you've got to send a message that says, "I'm somebody, because God made me somebody."

We're talking here about an inner strength that makes you attractive when you walk into a room, and causes others to ask, "Who's that?" And they won't be asking because your appearance is so stunning, but because your character is magnetic and your presence has impact.

This is not pride—it's just healthy self-esteem based on God's opinion of you. When you have it, it affects the way you ... talk to others ... sit in a classroom ... apply for a job ... perform the ministry God gave you ... and even how you pray. That's right; if you think you have no value, you'll pray with less faith, and conclude that the promises of God are for everybody but you.

Line up your opinion with God's! Appreciate who He made you to be, and develop what He gave you. Stop wishing you were somebody else. You are a unique blend of gifts and character. You have a special destiny on earth. You are somebody, because God loves you—remember that!

When you begin to understand that God loves you

unconditionally, you'll be able to accept yourself as you are, and accept others as they are too.

Stop and ask yourself today, "How do I really feel about myself?"

Before you answer, read these ten principles. Better yet, put them somewhere where you can read them every day.

(1) Never think or speak negatively about yourself, for that puts you in disagreement with God.

(2) Meditate on your strengths and learn to encourage yourself—for most of the time, nobody else will.

(3) Don't compare yourself to anybody else. You are unique, one-of-a-kind, an original, so don't settle for being a copy.

(4) Focus on your potential, not your limitations. Remember, God lives in you!

(5) Find something you like and do well, and strive to do it with excellence.

(6) Have the courage to be different; be a God-pleaser, not a people-pleaser.

(7) Learn to handle criticism; let it develop you instead of discourage you.

(8) Determine your own worth— before others do it for you.

(9) Keep your shortcomings in perspective—you're still a work in progress.

(10) Focus daily on your greatest source of confidence—God!

Chapter Three

Conquer Your Fear

Florence Chadwick, the first woman to swim the English Channel, failed on her first attempt, even though she was only half-a-mile from the shore when she quit. What stopped her? The fog! It dropped like a curtain, and a voice within her whispered, "You'll never make it." When they pulled her into the boat moments later, and she discovered how close she'd been to her goal, she broke down and wept. But she didn't quit. Instead she tried it again—and set a new world record in the process!

Are the same voices telling you today, "You'll never make it?" Take another look at the word F.E.A.R. It just means False Evidence Appearing Real!

My friend, Sarah Utterbach, says, "If you destroy the negative, the picture can never be developed." She's right! Fear is just the darkroom where all of our negatives are developed.

Most of my fears fall into two categories: (1) Fear that I won't get what I need; (2) Fear that I'll lose what I have got. Sound familiar?

Two of the biggest fears we face are criticism and rejection. If we let them, they can stop us dead in our tracks every time!

Have you noticed how often "They" decide what's important for us, and what's not? For example, "They" say that the chairman of the board is important, but the janitor's not. If you buy into that nonsense, you'll become insecure, resentful, and competitive. You'll also strive to become what "They" approve of, and miss your true calling in the process. Or worse, you'll actually do what God has called you to do, but never experience any fulfillment, because "They" planted so much self-doubt in your mind. Refuse to live that way another day!

It takes courage to be led by God's Spirit. It's not easy to break the mold in a family, or step outside the boundaries others have created for you. When you do, you'll face criticism. Jesus did. When they said,

"Is not this the carpenter's son ... ?" (Matthew 13:55), they were really saying, "He should stay in his place." Look out, they'll say that about you too!

Paul writes in Ephesians 6:6, "Not with eye service, as men pleasers; but as servants of Christ, doing the will of God from the heart."

Recently, somebody sent me the story of an old farmer and his grandson who owned a mule called Hiney. Things weren't going well on the farm, so they decided to take Hiney to town and sell him. As they started walking toward town, a woman saw them and shouted, "Why are you walking when you have a mule you could ride?" "Good point," they thought, so they both climbed on. A little further down the road another woman shouted to them, "With the weight of both of you on his back, he'll become exhausted." So the old man got off. Further down the road a man shouted, "Young man, how dare you make your old grandfather walk while you ride. You should be ashamed!" So, the boy got off, and the grandfather got back on. A little later somebody else shouted, "That poor mule looks like he's going to drop dead any minute. You both need to carry him for awhile." Thinking this was a good idea, they hoisted Hiney up on their shoulders, and started off again toward town. But, as they crossed a bridge, they lost their footing, and the mule dropped into the river and drowned.

What's the point of this story? Simply this—when you try to please everybody, you can lose your Hiney!

Remember, there are two kinds of people who always fail—those who listen to nobody and those who listen to everybody!

Paul says, "Each of us will give an account of himself to God" (Romans 14:12 NIV). In the end, you'll answer to Him alone. In that day, you'll discover that not only is it wrong to be judgmental, it's equally wrong to let the opinions of others control you or cause you to disobey God and miss your destiny.

You can have the most expensive car on the road, but if you don't know how to take the wheel or apply the brakes, it'll never get you where you need to go. Sure, it's nice to let others do the driving sometimes, but that puts you at the mercy of their direction. Take control of your life! Get back into the driver's seat and take the wheel, for only you know where God has told you to go.

Too often our actions are dictated not by a sense of purpose, but by a need to please. We care so much about what certain people think that with every step, we look over our shoulder to see whether they're smiling or frowning.

God says, "You shall have no other gods before me" (Exodus 20:3 NIV). "But I don't worship idols," you say. You do when you dedicate your life to impressing people instead of obeying God.

"But who am I to assert myself?" you ask. Who are you not to? You're a child of God, and as such, your first responsibility is to please Him. Your second is to live your life to the fullest.

Anybody who ever beat the odds or made a difference did it in spite of their fear. They did it because: (a) they were desperate and felt like they'd no choice; (b) they were inspired by somebody else's example; (c) they were angry at injustice; (d) they were moved by the need; (e) they said, "If not me, who? If not now, when?" (f) they didn't think much about it at all, or they might have changed their mind.

What are you waiting for? A feeling of courage? Forget it; it doesn't exist! You're only courageous when you do what's right—despite your fears! And since every one of us feels fear, then every one of us is capable of acting courageously. It's a choice!

Any time you go where you've never been or try what you've never done, fear will be present. But each time you conquer it, you gain self-respect, and a new level of confidence.

Peter didn't walk on the water because Jesus lifted him out of the boat and moved his legs for him. No, the miracle only happened because he responded to the Word. (See Matthew 24:29.)

How do you walk on water? (1) By seeing Jesus in your storm. (2) By obeying what He tells you to do. (3) By refusing to be intimidated by your surroundings. (4) By doing what others in the boat are afraid to do. (5) By believing what's possible, instead of settling for what's rational. All God needs is something to work with, and somebody to work through, and the rest, as they say, "is history!"

The only thing that will stop God from working on your behalf is unbelief. Listen, "And he did not do many miracles there because of their lack of faith. (Matthew 13: 58 NIV). Since God cannot be pleased without faith, you need to make a commitment today to developing your faith. Once you do that, the future's yours.

One day on a ferryboat, George Mueller, who was known for his extraordinary faith, prayed, "Lord, lift this fog so that I can get to church in time to speak." As he said, "Amen," and rose to his feet, the captain shouted, "Look—the fog's lifting!" Muller replied, "Just as I thought!"

Jesus said, "Therefore I tell you, whatever you ask for in prayer, believe that you have received it, and it will be yours" (Mark 11:24 NIV).

My sister Ruth has a cat named Charlie, who loves to defend his turf. And he does pretty well at it too, except for his old nemesis, a neighborhood cat called George! Early in the game, George learned that all he had to do was show up, let out a bloodcurdling wail, and Charlie breaks the four-minute mile!

That's how fear works. Suddenly, you find yourself in a state of near panic, confronted by old adversaries you've already conquered. Now you're afraid of the next phone call, or what might come in the mail, or what's around the next corner.

Like Elijah when he heard the voice of Jezebel, you're ready to run to the nearest cave and forget every victory God's ever given you.

Don't run anymore! God's put an arsenal at your disposal. Listen, "... when the day of evil comes [and it will] ... stand your ground ... take up the shield of faith, with which you can extinguish all the flaming arrows of the evil one ... and the sword of the Spirit, which is the Word of God" (Ephesians 6:13-17 NIV). Did you get that? Faith is your shield, the Word of God is your sword, and the enemy has no defense against either.

Peter writes, "Be self-controlled and alert. Your enemy [fear] prowls around like a roaring lion looking for someone to devour" (1 Peter 5:8 NIV).

I'm told that when a lion gets too old to hunt, it roars. It works like this: while the younger lions hide in the bushes off to one side, the old lion roars from the other, and their terrified prey in the middle runs from the roar—right into the trap!

Today, run to the roar! Confront your fears, and you'll discover that they have no power over you.

Chapter Four

Start Small

Everything big starts with something small. All God needs is something to start with!

Have you ever noticed what the disciples said to Jesus just before He fed the 5,000? Listen, "There is a lad here which hath five barley loaves and two small fishes: but what are they amongst so many?" (John 6:9). Is that how you feel today; the challenge is too big, and you're too small?

Notice, the miracle only began when they took what they had and put it into His hands. As long as you try to claim it or control it, it'll always be limited. But the moment you make it available to Him, it'll begin to grow! Imagine; just a boy's lunch; just a shepherd's staff—all God needs is something to start with.

The prophet Zechariah wrote, "Do not despise this small beginning, for the eyes of the Lord rejoice to see the work begin" (Zechariah 4:10 TLB). Don't be afraid to take small steps. Just make them steps of faith, and God will work with you.

In the day of small things, you learn God's ways, grow in wisdom, and develop faith for the big battles ahead.

Jesus said, "I will build my church ..." (Matthew 16:18). "Build it with what?" you ask. Twelve people just like you! But when He poured Himself into them, He was so concentrated in them, that if two of them got together, they could turn any town upside-down.

"But I have so many weaknesses," you say. We all come to the Lord damaged and in need of repair. The good news is, you can be strong in certain areas and struggling in others, yet God will still use you.

Paul says, "God's gifts and His call are irrevocable" (Romans 11:29 NIV). God never removes His gifts from your life! Samson's gift of strength finally destroyed him, but he never lost it. Even if you haven't discovered your gift yet, or you're running from it, or you feel like you've abused it— you still have it!

God's gifts are never loans; they're deposits, and as such, they're never used up or depleted. The more you exercise them, the stronger they become.

I remember my own early struggles in the ministry. I felt like I was stuck in an elevator—afraid I'd spend the rest of my life between floors, going nowhere. Yet it was concern over the future, plus my fear of failing, that kept me on my knees. That's where I developed a prayer life. That's where I learned to depend on God.

My first pastorate was in the village of Back Bay, New Brunswick, in Canada. I was barely twenty-five, and my congregation consisted of 250 sardine packers and lobster fishermen.

The old wooden church overlooked the Bay of Fundy and had a steeple with a bell tower, which I rang vigorously every Sunday morning. The message was simple; "You may not come to church—but you won't sleep either!"

For six years I had traveled as an evangelist, speaking an average of six nights a week in different churches. During that time I perfected a basic repertoire of about twenty sermons, which I'd preached so often that had I dropped dead in the middle of any one of them, my wife could have finished it!

But now I was facing the challenge of preparing three new sermons each week, and I'd only have one shot at each of them. Could I do it? Could I stay fresh?

Grow with my congregation? Build a strong pulpit? Those were the fears I had as we unpacked our meager belongings, and moved into the parsonage next door to the church.

Looking back I can see God's wisdom at work. He placed me in a small community where I could do the least amount of damage while I was learning!

I'd preached my first sermon at the age of thirteen in Belfast, Ireland. But since I had never had an opportunity to attend seminary, I was painfully aware of my lack of formal training. I did, however, have two great mentors—Dr. Gordon Magee and Dr. James McConnell. The first instructed me, and the second inspired me. It's a good way to learn, for in the final analysis, ministry is not taught; it's caught!

But now I'd been thrown into the deep end! My well-polished sermons had earned me an invitation, a parsonage, a car allowance, and seventy-five dollars a week. The question now was—did I have what it took?

Every weekend the challenge came back. By Tuesday the pressure began to build as I approached Sunday. Often I'd study until 2:00 or 3:00 A.M. on Sunday morning and leave my office feeling drained and apprehensive, praying, "Lord, if you don't help me tomorrow, I'm sunk."

But I learned to swim. I became a reader, discovered great sources, developed discipline and solid study habits, and above all, learned to lean on God as never before. When I left there two years later, the congregation had multiplied, and we had completed a beautiful new building.

Paul speaks about, "… the exceeding greatness of His power to us-ward who believe" (Ephesians 1:19).

The Bible is a "David and Goliath" book. It teaches you that with God on your side, all you need is a rag and a rock, and you're bigger than any problem. The question is, do you believe that enough to step out, allow God to use you, and put yourself in the place of total dependence on Him?

If you're just believing God for things you can do for yourself, you're limiting Him. Why? Because His Word says, "… the eyes of the Lord run to and fro throughout the whole earth, to show Himself strong in the behalf of them whose heart is perfect toward Him" (2 Chronicles 16:9).

If your vision of the future is truly from God, it'll stretch you beyond your present resources. Actually, the difference between your vision and your resources is your opportunity to experience the "exceeding greatness of His power" (Ephesians 1:19).

Furthermore, if you think He'll never ask you to do what you can't do, think again! Jesus told one man to walk on water and another to come out of his grave—and they did!

I can tell you from forty years of walking with God that when you find yourself experiencing things which are beyond your ability—that's when you know God's at work, demonstrating the exceeding greatness of His power.

"But I'm only one person," you say. With God, one person is a majority.

In 1858, a Boston Sunday school teacher named Kimball began visiting one of his students at the shoe store where he worked as a clerk. Eventually, he led him to Christ. That student's name was D.L. Moody. Twenty-one years later, Moody, now an evangelist, visited London, and a great spiritual awakening took place. F.B. Meyer, a local pastor, went to hear Moody preach, and his life was transformed. Later Meyer went to America to speak, and in one of his meetings a student called J. Wilbur Chapman came to Christ. Chapman became active in the YMCA, where he met and discipled a former baseball player named Billy Sunday. Sunday became a great revivalist, and in one of his crusades in Charlotte, North Carolina, a group of businessmen were won to Christ. A year later they decided that their city needed another crusade, so they invited Mordecai Hamm, a Baptist evangelist, to be their speaker. After three weeks, Hamm left town, discouraged because he'd only made one convert, a twelve-year-old boy called— Billy Graham. And the rest is history!

One Sunday school teacher started it all! One brother, Andrew, led another brother called Peter, to Christ; but Peter brought multitudes. One woman, whose name he still doesn't know, led Dr. David Yonggi-Cho, pastor of the world's largest church (800,000 members), to Christ.

One person—just one—can make all the difference!

Chapter Five

Discover Your Calling

In the movie City Slickers, Billy Crystal plays a city guy on vacation out West, and Jack Palance plays the part of a crusty old cowboy who entertains him. One conversation goes like this:

Palance: "How old are you?"

Crystal: "Thirty-nine."

Palance: "Yeah, you all come out here about the same age. Same problems; spend fifty weeks a year getting knots in your rope, and think two weeks up here will untie them for you. None of you get it. Do you know what the secret of life is?"

Crystal: "No, what?"

Palance: "One thing. Just one thing—you stick to that, and everything else don't mean nuthin'."

Crystal: "That's great, but what's the one thing?"

Palance: "That's for you to figure out!"

The old cowboy was right—you've got to figure out the "one thing" you were born to be, and be willing to pay the price to be it.

Paul writes, "… let's just go ahead and be what we were made to be, without … comparing ourselves with each other, or trying to be something we aren't. If you preach, just preach God's message, nothing else; if you help, just help, don't take over. If you teach, stick to your teaching; if you give encouraging guidance, be careful that you don't get bossy; if you're put in charge, don't manipulate; if you're called to give aid to people in distress, keep your eyes open and be quick to respond; if you work with the disadvantaged, don't let yourself get irritated with them or depressed by them. Keep a smile on your face. Love from the center of who you are; don't fake it" (Romans 12:5-9 TM).

Notice the words, "let's just go ahead and be what we were meant to be." Don't let anybody label you! Don't let them put you in a box!

It's amazing; the moment we're born, somebody decides that this little wrinkly, toothless, bald baby "looks exactly like so and so." Then later they say, "Well, he's just a 'C' student." Or, "She's just a plain Jane." Before you know it, you grow up believing that stuff and sell yourself short because somebody labeled you!

Paul said to Timothy, "Don't let anyone look down on you because you are young" (1 Timothy 4:12 NIV). And let's add … because you're poor, or uneducated, or physically challenged, or of a certain nationality, or because of a mistake in your past. Don't let them label you!

Adam Clark was a renowned preacher in 18th Century England. Yet when he was a boy, his father told his schoolteacher that he didn't think his son would do too well in school. "He looks very bright to me," the teacher replied. Those words changed Adam Clark's life. They released him from the box his father had put him in. He lived to be seventy-two, became one of the most gifted ministers in his generation, and gave the world one of its finest sets of Bible commentaries.

Get rid of your life-limiting thoughts! Start dreaming! When God defines you, what difference does anybody else's opinion make?

You were born with an assignment; don't die until you've fulfilled it. Your God-given assignment will always: (a) tug at your heart; (b) lead to your highest fulfillment; (c) and unlock your compassion and creativity. Whether He's called you to be a butcher, a baker, or a candlestick maker, those principles never change; they're timeless.

When God calls you to do something, He prepares you in advance. By the time I preached my first sermon, I had been steeped in church, and all my heroes were preachers. At the time I saw no way to get from the lowly pew where I sat to the pulpit I admired so much. Yet God had created within me a desire for ministry; and desire is always the first step towards destiny!

Take a look at how God prepared Moses, and maybe you'll understand how He works in our lives.

First, He'll give you an emotional investment in the work He's called you to do. How ironic; Pharaoh ordered the death of every Hebrew male under two, yet he was raising one in his own palace who would liberate the children of Israel and bring down his entire kingdom.

The Israelites were not some unknown group; they were Moses' own people. Their cries had echoed in his ears for forty years, and now he was willing to lay down his life for them. That's what it takes to be used by God—an emotional investment!

Second, He begins with your character, then He works on your calling. Usually He does this in obscurity. In the case of Moses, God spent forty years tearing down the old building and reconstructing it from the ground up.

Those years in the wilderness must have seemed like forever. Yet it was during this time that Moses encountered God in a fire that wasn't dependent on him, because God started it and God sustained it.

It was there that he learned to discern the voice of God from every other voice. Think of the value of that, when a-hundred-and-one different people start giving you their opinions! It was there that he developed faith to receive manna from heaven, water from a rock, and a way through The Red Sea.

Third, He never wastes experience! If Moses hadn't been raised in the palace, Pharaoh would probably have viewed him as some crazy shepherd with a bad case of sunstroke and had him killed immediately. But his past positioned him for his future. Also because of his desert training, he was able to feed, clothe, protect, and lead an entire nation through the Sinai wasteland. The fact that he'd been born into the home of Hebrew slaves gave him the compassion and the vision to say yes to such a task.

Bill Hybels, pastor of the 25,000-member Willow Creek Church in Illinois, tells of laboring as a teenager in his father's produce business. One day he and his brother had to unload a huge trailer-full of potatoes that had gone bad. Even though they had no forklift or palate jack, they managed to unload the entire forty foot trailer—one bag of rotten potatoes at a time. In the process, Hybels learned two important lessons. First, he learned that even impossible tasks can be accomplished if you keep doing one thing at a time. Second, he learned that it's the practice of systematically doing the right things that yields results over time.

Fourth, before others can catch a vision, it must be born in the heart of one person. Before a single Hebrew slave caught the vision of The Promised Land, Moses saw men and women no longer bound by chains, building their own homes, tending their own crops, and worshipping in their own temple.

But how did he keep his vision alive in a wilderness of adversity? Listen, "He persevered because he saw him who is invisible" (Hebrews 11:27). He was sustained by what he saw—and your vision will sustain you too!

Over a century ago David Livingston read these words by Robert Moffat: "From where I stand, I can see the smoke of 10,000 African villages that have never heard of Christ."

Like an encounter with a burning bush, those words ignited a vision in Livingston's heart. As a result, he traveled 11,000 miles on foot through uncharted jungles. He was racked by disease, attacked by wild animals, menaced by hostile tribes, and even robbed by his own carriers. Yet he marched on with his Bible. He preached the Gospel and fought slavery until he won the heart of a nation and planted the seeds of emancipation in both Britain and America.

On May 1, 1873, he was found dead on his knees in a dilapidated hut in an obscure African village—all because he had a dream!

Fifth, God will never give you a vision you can fulfill alone. He'll bring others alongside to compensate for your weaknesses. He gave Joshua to Moses to be his personal assistant. He gave him Aaron and Hur to hold up his hands so that the battle could be won. He gave him Jethro, his father-in-law, to save him from a leader's most dreaded fate—death by administration (Exodus 18:25-26). Finally, He gave him seventy elders who caught his spirit and enabled him to complete the job (Numbers 11:16).

Moses changed his life at forty, and found his destiny at eighty. So it's not over until God says it's over! Max Lucado says, "If God can speak from a burning bush to a shepherd called Moses, then He can speak from a mop bucket to a janitor called Hank." God knows what you're being trained for, and when the time is right He'll make it clear to you. In the meantime, stay in school and keep learning, otherwise you'll never graduate.

Had you seen Moses at forty years old you'd have said, "Surely he's the man for the job." Educated by royalty, trained by generals, and with instant access to Pharaoh. But you'd have been wrong! The eighty year-old Moses may smell like a shepherd and speak like a farmer, but he's God's choice!

Dick Berry was a real estate salesman when God gave him the vision of putting the first Christian radio station on the air in New Zealand. At the time, the circumstances seemed impossible.

For seventeen years he prayed and persevered, until finally the government gave him a one-day, low-power license. The signal was so weak it barely traveled a few blocks. Yet, it was the breakthrough he'd been praying for.

Before he died at forty-four, God used him to give

birth to the first Christian Broadcasting Network in the British Commonwealth, and lay the foundation for one of the world's fastest growing missionary networks—United Christian Broadcasters International.

Stop trying to be what you're not, and discover what you are. Instead of comparing yourself to others, recognize what God has called you to be, accept the gifts He's given you, and start building on them.

Chapter Six

Set High Standards

D id you hear about the woman who was such a terrible housekeeper that Good Housekeeping cancelled her subscription? Seriously, Paul writes, "Let all things be done decently and in order" (1 Corinthians 14:40). Now while most of us don't struggle with being decent, we do struggle with being orderly. We squander valuable time and energy because we're not better organized. If you want to test yourself in this area, answer these ten questions:

(1) How often do you lose things? (2) Are you usually late or on time? (3) Do you procrastinate? (4) Are your big time-wasters telephone and television? (5) Do you pay your bills on time? (6) Do you return

telephone calls and answer your mail promptly—or at all? (7) Do you have lots of unfinished projects lying around? (8) Can you locate important documents right away? (9) Do you have a current will, in a safe place, where it can be found? (10) Do you think things through?

Well, how'd you do?

If you really want to put order into your life, start by writing down the habits you need to work on. Don't announce, "Starting today, everybody 'round here is gonna change." No, work on yourself first, and only work on one or two things at a time. If you try to shoot at too many targets, you'll hit none and give up in discouragement.

A big insurance company recently conducted a work-study, during which they discovered that twenty percent of their employees did eighty percent of the work. That meant the other eighty percent only did twenty percent of the work. But they found something even more interesting—the twenty percent at the top produced sixteen percent more than the eighty percent at the bottom. Did that mean they were smarter or more experienced? No, it just meant they'd chosen to be the best by committing to excellence on the job.

What kind of worker are you? Do you pull your

weight? Are you a clock-watcher? Do you depend on others to carry you? Do you think that your working conditions are tough and your job demeaning?

Jesus clearly taught excellence in all that we do. Listen, "In a word, what I'm saying is, grow up. You're kingdom subjects. Now live like it. Live out your God-created identity" (Matthew 5:48 TM). Your work is a self-portrait of the one who does it, so, make sure you autograph it with excellence.

Part of setting high standards for yourself is making a commitment to being honest regardless of the circumstances. Solomon said, "Better to be poor and honest than a rich person no one can trust" (Proverbs 19:1 TM).

The other day I heard a man refer to the story of Ananias and Sapphira in Acts, Chapter 5. He said, "I'm glad God doesn't strike people dead today for lying." Don't be so sure. The wages of deceit are still death; maybe not physical death, but the death of other things like: (a) Your marriage: Lies in a marriage are like termites in a tree; it may survive for years, but inevitably it will fall, destroying other things in its path. (b) Your conscience: The first lie you tell makes you a liar, not the fiftieth. After that, each successive one just tightens the knot and strengthens the rope that binds you. (c) Your career: Ask the student who just got expelled for cheating or the worker who was just fired for embezzling if it was worth it?

And what about the death of trust, intimacy, peace of mind, and integrity? When you live on two different levels, you not only lose respect for yourself, you also lose your confidence before God, and your moral authority before the world. Simply stated, the rewards are just not worth it.

Paul says that, "We should be holy and without blame before Him" (Ephesians 1:4).

The word holiness is a turn-off to a lot of people. They immediately think of all the things you can't do—like a religious version of Robert's Rules of Order. Nothing could be further from the truth. Listen again, "He hath chosen us ... that we should be holy [fully committed]" (Ephesians 1:4). You'll never have the motivation to live a fully committed lifestyle, unless you know God has chosen you for a specific purpose.

It's like being an athlete—certain activities may be permissible for others, but not for you, because you want to win.

Notice the words, "We should be holy before Him." Holiness just means being constantly aware of what pleases and what offends God.

In the Old Testament, God used forks, spoons, basins, and flesh hooks for temple worship. Now, they were just ordinary forks, spoons, basins, and flesh hooks until He set them aside for His use. Then, they became holy forks, holy spoons, holy basins, and holy flesh hooks. Since contamination could disqualify them for service, they had to be protected.

And it's the same with you. When God called you, He earmarked you for a specific purpose. Before, you were just Fred and Helen. But now you're holy Fred and holy Helen. Like the dedicated line on a fax machine, you can be used for one thing only—His purposes. Once you understand that and accept it, you'll never stray far from His will.

To excel at anything, you have to make trade-off's. Here are three of the biggest:

(1) Immediate pleasure for personal growth. It takes decades to grow an oak tree, but only days to grow a squash. Which do you want to be? Are you willing to discipline yourself in order get there?

(2) Everything for one thing. When you're young, it's good to experiment. But once you've discovered God's purpose for your life, pay the required price, give it all you've got, and refuse to be sidetracked.

(3) Quantity for quality. You don't really pay for

things with money—you pay with time. For example, we say, "In seven years I'll have enough to build my dream home; then I'll slow down." But seven years could be one-tenth of your life! Is it worth that? Always translate the dollar value of everything into time, and you'll know whether or not it's for you.

John Maxwell gives us the following formula for making our lives count: "Give God the first part of every day, the first day of every week, the first portion of every paycheck, and the first consideration in every decision."

That's a formula that can't fail.

Chapter Seven

Know What Season You're In

For twenty years, I had the privilege to travel and speak in some of the world's finest churches. Even though it was draining, and I was on the road forty-five weekends out of every year, God gave me the "grace" to do it, so it was rewarding and enjoyable.

But a few years ago that season ended, and God changed my direction. Today my greatest joy is to stay home and write The Word For You Today, a daily devotional currently read by over one million people, in twenty different languages.

For ten years I enjoyed considerable success as a fund-raiser at Christian telethons. One weekend, at the invitation of my friend Jerry Rose, I went to

Channel 38 in Chicago, where we raised the highest amount ever pledged in a single weekend. Yet, when I went back the following year, I could barely raise one-tenth of that amount. As I walked off the set exhausted, a voice inside me confirmed what I had known for some time, "Your season for this has ended."

Life's like that—it's lived on levels and in seasons.

"How can I tell when a season is ending?" you ask. Because the grace that accompanied that season is no longer there, and what was once easy is now hard.

David said that a successful man or woman is like a tree planted by streams of water, "… which yields its fruit in season" (Psalms 1:3 NIV). You can only be fruitful in your season! That's where blessing and success occur. You can't just do it whenever you want to. It has to be in your appointed time. (Ecclesiastes 3:1). When the right season comes, it's effortless for a tree to produce what's stored within.

There's fruit within you that can only be successfully produced when you understand what season you're in. There are rules for each:

Spring is for training and discipline. That's when you begin to see God's purpose for your life, and prepare for it. Summer is for maturing what Spring started. Whatever you nurtured then, good or bad, will grow and multiply now. Autumn is when you no longer have the passion of youth, but the stately calm of the seasoned veteran. If you're wise, you're now working smarter, not harder. It's time to transition and prepare for the upcoming winter. Winter is when you assess your accomplishments, enjoy your assets, pass on your counsel, and take your bows. You have fought the good fight, kept the faith, and finished the course.

If you do it right, each season can be the best one of your life.

Jesus said, "Every branch in me that beareth not fruit He taketh away: and every branch that beareth fruit, He purgeth it, that it may bring forth more fruit" (John 15:2). There's a time for planting, and a time for pruning.

God may be at work in your life today, taking away the branches that don't belong and pruning the ones that do.

"What kinds of things does He take away?" you ask. Things that have served their purpose ... things that refuse to change ... things that will give you trouble later on ... things that are standing in the way of something better ... things that are holding you back ... things He has not chosen for you!

Have you ever seen a newly-pruned tree? Doesn't look too good, does it?

When God starts to cut back certain things in your life in order to redirect your energies, you won't look too good either. Sometimes this means: (1) having fewer things for a while; (2) letting go of things you thought would always be there; (3) being unable to explain to others why you're even going through this.

God knows what needs to be cut back in your life; He also knows what needs to be cut off. Trust Him! Even when you can't understand it, just pray, "Lord, if I needed it, You would let me keep it; so I open my hand to You today. Send whenever You will, and take away whenever You will. I'll praise You when they come, and I'll praise You when they go, because my hope is built on nothing less than Jesus' blood and righteousness."

Waiting is not easy—yet it's necessary. The prophet Habakkuk wrote, "Though it linger, wait for it; it will certainly come" (Habakkuk 2:3 NIV).

God works on both ends of the line. He gets you ready for it (even when you don't know what "it" is), and He gets it ready for you. You could be called to pastor, yet while you're waiting, have to sweep out the church or drive the Sunday school bus—and not lose your self-esteem in the process.

Look at Joshua; he's been to the Promised Land and tasted its blessings. But now he has to go back and live with people who have no idea— and in most cases, no interest—in what he's talking about. Is that where you are today? Have you been asking, "Lord, how long will my passion be there, but my place be here? How long do I have to keep this promise in my heart, and not have a soul to share it with?"

Wait! Your appointment is still on God's calendar. Listen, "There has never been the slightest doubt in my mind that the God who started this great work in you would keep at it and bring it to a flourishing finish" (Philippians 1:6 TM). Even though your promise may be postdated— remember whose signature is on the check!

To get from where you are to where you're going, you have to be willing to be in-between. It's hard to let go of the familiar and stand with your hands empty while you wait for God to fill them. Especially in the areas of:

(a) Feelings. You can actually become comfortable with feelings of anger and resentment. When you finally face them and decide to let them go, you can feel empty for a time; this is normal. You're in between pain and the peace that comes from forgiving and accepting. Hang in there—it will pass.

(b) Relationships. When you let someone go (even from a bad relationship), it can be frightening because now you're feeling a sense of loss. Don't rush into another relationship half-dressed and ill-prepared. Wait! Talk to God. You need this time to become whole and learn to make healthier choices.

(c) Jobs, homes, and goals. You've let go of the old, but you're not sure whether you can handle the new—or if it's even going to come. David said, "Weeping may endure for a night, but joy cometh in the morning" (Psalm 30:5). Did you hear that? Joy is on the way! But until it arrives, hold steady and trust God to know what He's doing.

When Jesus said to His disciples, "Let us go over to the other side ... " (Matthew 4:35 NIV), the lessons they learned and the miracles they experienced in between changed them forever.

And they'll change you too!

Chapter Eight

Follow Your Dream

G od loves dreamers. He's the giver of new dreams and the mender of broken ones.

When you dream, you move closer to the way He sees things. In that moment, you rise above your limitations; you move from where you are to where He wants you to be. In other words, you begin to see your goals in their completed state.

The question is not can you dream, but do you have the courage to act on it? If faith without works is dead, then a dream without diligence is dead too. (James 2:20). God won't miraculously lift you out of your dream and set you down in the middle of its fulfillment. Thoreau said, "It's fine to build castles in the air, so long as you work to put foundations under them."

The children of Israel dreamed of The Promised Land, but the only way to get there was through the wilderness. That's where they learned to: (a) trust God daily for what they needed; (b) discover His power in "The Red Sea situations" of life; (c) learn how to be led by Him; (d) keep their eyes on their destiny and move steadily toward it; and (e) refuse to become like those who murmur, complain, and never make it.

William Carey was called "a dreamer" because he studied foreign languages and the travel-logs of Captain Cook. Those who knew him when he was just a cobbler scoffed at the big map he kept on the wall of his workshop, so that he could pray for the nations every day. One night after he'd spoken at a conference on the subject, "Is the great commission for today?" an older minister got up and publicly rebuked him, saying, "If God wants to convert the heathen, He'll do it without your help or mine." Carey was silenced for the moment—but not stopped.

Before he died, William Carey took the Gospel to India and became the father of modern missions!

When you begin to pursue your dream, somebody will always emerge to try and steal it. Often it'll be someone who never had a dream of their own, or if they did, they abandoned it. It could even be a family member, who constantly reminds you of what God couldn't or wouldn't do through someone like you.

What do you dream about? What has God enabled you to see, which does not yet exist? You'll never out-dream God! Listen, "God can do ... far more than you can ever imagine or guess or request in your wildest dreams!" (Ephesians 3:20 TM).

Robert Lopatin thought it was too late for him. As a boy he'd dreamed of becoming a doctor, but instead, when he graduated from college, he went into his father's hardware business. Twenty years later when his father sold out, Robert had the option of retiring. But he couldn't.

One day at a friend's wedding, he talked to a young medical school graduate and suddenly remembered his boyhood dream.

At 51, he decided to go back to school to become a doctor. It took enormous commitment, but he did it. At 56, he graduated from New York's Einstein College of Medicine, and now works at a medical center in the Bronx. He loves it—even the 100-hour weeks and the graveyard shifts! He says, "I feel like I died and was born again."

Is there a dream in your heart? Has life buried it? Have others told you it's too late? Don't you believe it! Robert Lopatin became a doctor in his mid-fifties. Grandma Moses took up painting when she was seventy-five and had a celebrated twenty-six-year career as an artist. Noah started building the ark at five hundred.

Pursue your dream no matter how farfetched it may seem, for dreams are like your children; they're your offspring. They're the joy of your present and the hope of your future. Protect them! Feed them! Encourage them to grow, for as long as you have a dream—you'll never be old!

In spite of betrayal by his family, repeated attempts at seduction by Potiphar's wife, and false imprisonment, Joseph's dream carried him all the way to his destiny as ruler of Egypt.

We're talking here about a God-given dream that leads to God-honoring results. Paul writes, "Long before we heard of Christ ... He had ... designs on us for glorious living" (Ephesians 1:11 TM). Did you hear that? God has a dream for you, and if you seek Him, He'll reveal it to you. But when He does, remember three things:

(1) Dreams are specific, not general; personal, not

public. God won't give somebody else your dream, He'll give it to you. He may confirm it through others, but He'll reveal it to you first. When He does, don't share it with the wrong people or you'll get hurt. Like Joseph's brothers, they won't be able to handle it.

(2) Dreams are usually outside the realm of the expected. Often they'll cause rational people to look at you and say, "You've got to be kidding!" Before God does the miraculous, He may ask you to do the ridiculous. Are you prepared for that?

(3) Dreams separate leaders from followers. Dreamers are always a minority. Those who live by sight will always outnumber those who live by faith.

So today, follow your God-given dream!

Chapter Nine

Persevere

One of my favorite stories is the story of a farmer whose mule fell into a well. Since there was no way to get him out, the farmer decided to bury him there. But the mule had a different idea. Initially, when the shovels of dirt started landing on his back, he became hysterical. Then this thought struck him: "Just shake it off, and step on it." So he did. Hour after hour, as the dirt fell on him, he kept telling himself, "Just shake it off, and step on it!"

No matter how much dirt they threw on him, he just kept shaking it off and stepping on it until finally he stepped triumphantly out of the well.

Life will either bury you or bless you; the

difference lies in having the right attitude. Paul had it. Listen, "In all these things we are more than conquerors ..." (Romans 8:37). When they throw dirt on you—and they will—just shake it off, and use it as fertilizer and grow stronger.

Jesus said, "Offenses will come ..." (Luke 17:1). So expect them. People will take from you without ever giving back. They'll criticize you for simply rising above your beginnings. When you decide to seize the moment and move ahead, you'll leave others behind—and some of them won't be too happy about it. The only way to avoid that is to do nothing and stay where you are!

Eleanor Roosevelt once said, "No one can make you feel inferior without your consent." You see, what's important is not what others say about you, but what you say about yourself after they get through talking. Kenneth Tynan says, "Critics are people who think they know the way; the problem is, they can't drive the car." When you understand that, it enables you to love them, forgive them, and keep moving ahead.

David said, "The righteous will flourish like a palm tree" (Psalms 92:12 NIV). If you need motivation, take another look at the palm tree.

(a) You can cut it, but you can't kill it. The minerals

and nutrients most trees need to survive are found just below the bark, so when you cut them they die. But not the palm tree. Its life comes from its heart, so it thrives even under attack.

(b) It bends, but it won't break. Tropical storms can blow most trees away, but not the palm tree. It's resilient. It bends all the way to the ground, yet when the storm is over, it straightens up again and is actually stronger in the place where it bent. You were made to bend and not break. The Bible says God gives us "… strength that endures the unendurable and spills over into joy" (Colossians 1:11 TM).

(c) Its depth always exceeds its height. While the roots of the average plant only go a few feet under, the roots of the palm tree go deep in search of water. David said, "As the deer panteth for streams of water, so my soul pants for you" (Psalms 42:1 NIV). Go deep. Stay connected to the streams and you'll never be uprooted, or barren, or blown away.

Chuck Swindoll writes, "Somebody needs to address the other side of Christian life. If for no other reason than to uphold reality, we need to be told that difficulty and pressure are par-for-the-course. No amount of biblical input, deeper life conferences, or super-victory seminars will exempt you from struggle. God promises no bubble of protection. Ask guys like

Job or Joseph, Daniel or Paul, and you'll become acquainted with an ancient word that has almost disappeared in this generation of splashy, always-grinning, a-miracle-a-day spirituality—perseverance. I know of no better partner to dance with when you're doing the three-steps-forward and two-steps-back number.

"It's in the tough times that true character is forged, the life of Christ is reproduced in us, and our flimsy theology is exchanged for a set of convictions that enable us to handle things, rather than trying to escape from them.

"It's when the bottom drops out, and life tries to pound you into a corner of doubt and unbelief, that you need what perseverance produces: (1) willingness to accept whatever comes, (2) determination to stand firm, and (3) insight to see God in it all. Without that, we stumble and fall, and God is grieved. With it, we survive and conquer, and God is glorified."

You may feel discouraged at the moment, but you're not finished. That only happens when you quit—and quitting isn't an option for you. Can you think of one quitter—just one—who ever accomplished anything worthwhile?

When John Wesley was forbidden to speak in a certain church, instead of giving up, he just went to a nearby cemetery where his father was buried, and using his tombstone as a pulpit, preached, and won souls to Christ.

John Knox, founder of the Presbyterian Church of Scotland, often had to be helped up the steps into the pulpit. But once there, he preached with such passion that the country turned to God!

One night George Whitefield returned extremely tired from a preaching tour. As he lit a candle and prepared to climb the stairs to his bedroom, he noticed a group of people gathered in front of his house. So he invited them into the foyer, and candle in hand, preached his last message from the stairway. That night he died in his sleep.

Storms come for a reason. They also come for a season. Discover the reason and become wiser. Outlast the season and become strong. But never quit!

William Blake said, "There's no mistake so great as the mistake of not going on!" Long before Alexander Graham Bell invented the telephone, a German schoolteacher named Reese almost did. Reese's phone could convey sounds of whistling and humming, but not speech. Something was missing. Many years later when Reese had given up, Bell discovered his error. A tiny screw that controlled the electrodes was off by one one-thousandth of an inch. When Bell made this minor adjustment, he was able to transmit speech loud and clear.

Think about it—an adjustment so small that you could barely measure it, spelled the difference between success and failure—and changed history!

There are two lessons in this: first it's the little things that open the door or close it—things like choosing kindness instead of criticism, cooperation instead of independence, discipline instead of impulsiveness. Little acts, little attitudes: they either work for you or against you. Second, if Reese had only persisted or reached for help—his name would be on the telephone today instead of Bell's.

Abraham Lincoln wrote, "Success is going from failure to failure without losing your enthusiasm." Elbert Hubbard wrote, "There is no defeat except in no longer trying; no really insurmountable barrier, save our own inherent weakness of purpose."

Charles Lindbergh said, "Success is not measured by what a man accomplishes, but by the opposition he encountered, and the courage he maintained in his struggle against it."

The University of Chicago conducted a five-year survey of The 20 Top-Performers in various fields, including music, athletics, art, mathematics, medicine, acting, and business. They also interviewed the families and teachers of the celebrated high achievers to find out how they did it. What they discovered was that drive and determination, not talent, led to their success. Imagine that, just plain, old stick-to-it-iveness!

Anybody who ever did anything worthwhile had it. The Master Teacher Himself gave us the formula for success when He said, "Staying with it—that's what God requires. Stay with it to the end. You won't be sorry" (Matthew 24:13 TM).

Chapter Ten

The Right Mind-set

When you entertain certain thoughts in the privacy of your own mind, you may be tempted to excuse yourself by saying, "What harm can it do?" A lot! Ultimately, you become whatever you meditate on! Solomon said, "For as he thinketh in his heart, so is he" (Proverbs 23:7).

When evil sets out to tear you down, it doesn't start with an act; it starts with a thought. Now thoughts are not yours just because they come into your mind. No, they only become yours when you allow them to move in and rearrange the furniture.

A thought left to ramble through your mind can attach itself to a weakness or an event in your past and feed on it. The stronger it grows, the weaker you become until finally all your strength is drained away. Don't let that happen to you. Paul writes, "Take captive every thought to make it obedient to Christ" (2 Corinthians 10:5 NIV). In other words, take your thoughts captive before they take you captive.

In Ephesians, chapter four, Paul writes, "Put off … the old man … put on the new man …" There are some old clothes you've got to take off when you commit yourself to a God-given goal—like old thinking patterns, old attitudes, and old behaviors. You may not even want to admit that you're still wearing those old clothes, but the truth is you can't put on the new man until you first take off the old one.

Furthermore, you can't hang those old clothes in a closet for a rainy day or leave them on the floor to be tripped over. You've got to get rid of them! Paul says, "Put away all falsehood and tell your neighbor the truth … don't let the sun go down while you are still angry, for anger gives a mighty foothold to the devil. If you are a thief, stop stealing. Begin using your hands for honest work … give generously to others in need. Don't use foul or abusive language. Let everything you say be … helpful so that your words will be an encouragement to those who hear them" (Ephesians 4:25-29 NLT).

"Is such a life-style possible?" you ask. Yes! Because God's Spirit lives in you, you don't have to: (a) lie to advance your position; (b) steal to be prosperous; (c) deceive to achieve; (d) use anger as a control mechanism; or (e) engage in corrupt communication.

When God tells you to take off the old and put on the new, He's talking about having the right mind-set. A big part of that is learning to be content. The Bible says, "… godliness with contentment is great gain" (1 Timothy 6:6). Now sometimes when you talk about contentment, people think you're against progress. No, Paul is simply saying that contentment never comes from externals. Never! The Greek sage said, "To whom little is not enough, nothing is ever enough."

Every twelve minutes television advertisers try to convince you that contentment is not possible without their particular brand of product. As you watch, you start to feel "less than" if you don't have it. So you go out and buy it, put yourself in debt, and miss out on what's truly important. Next time you see one of those commercials, just shout back at the TV, "Who-are-you-kidding?!?"

Get rid of the idea that "more is better." America has less than six percent of the world's population, but more than fifty percent of its wealth. Now, if more is better, we ought to be the happiest humans on the planet. But are we? You already know the answer to that!

The desire for more can be insatiable. As long as you believe that more is better, you'll never be satisfied because you'll never live long enough to have it all. Think, when you get something or achieve something, do you even take the time to enjoy it, or do you just move on to the next event without stopping?

After the Dalai Lama received the Nobel Peace Prize in New York City, a reporter asked him, "What's next?" That just about says it all, doesn't it?

The next time the "more is better" feeling hits you, immediately remind yourself that it doesn't work because the same mind-set that wants more now will want even more later.

If you don't want to get old too soon and smart too late, listen to what God has to say on this subject.

(1) "We didn't bring anything with us when we came into the world, and we certainly can't carry anything with us when we die" (1 Timothy 6:7 NLT). That verse explains why you never see a hearse pulling a U-haul trailer. It's a one-way trip. Furthermore, when you die and people ask, "How much did he leave?" The answer will be—everything!

(2) "And some people craving money, have wandered from the faith" (1 Timothy 6:10 NLT). If your pursuit of things leaves you no time for God, you're heading for trouble. Reexamine your priorities and start changing them.

(3) Solomon writes, "It is [good] for a man to enjoy his work, whatever his job may be ... the person who does that will not need to look back with sorrow on his past, for God gives him joy" (Ecclesiastes 5:18-20 LB).

Stop wishing your life away! Stop thinking, "If only I had a bigger house, a more understanding partner, a better-paying job, a more beautiful body, a higher IQ, or the acceptance of a particular person, I'd be happy. It doesn't work that way. The Bible says, "This is the day which the Lord hath made; we will rejoice and be glad in it" (Psalms 118:24). Did you hear that? Today, not tomorrow!

T.D. Jakes says his mother was a wonderful cook, and he loved to watch her bake. In his great book, Maximize the Moment, he writes, "With my fingers in the bowl and batter smudged across my cheeks, I learned what it later took me years to articulate—that all of life is good. If you want to enjoy it to the fullest, don't wait for what's in the oven, take the bowl now and get something out of every part."

Jesus said, "Look at the birds ..." (Matthew 6:26 NIV). "See how the lilies of the field grow" (Matthew 6:28). "Be content ..." (Luke 3:14). What is He saying? Simply this—take time to enjoy where you are on your way to where you're going.

If you feel like circumstances have you locked in today, read this:

"About midnight Paul and Silas were praying and singing hymns to God ... suddenly there was such a violent earthquake, that the foundations of the prison were shaken. At once all the prison doors flew open, and everybody's chains came loose" (Acts 16:25-26 NIV). Wow! When God taps His foot to the music, things happen!

The same power that opened every prison door for Paul and Silas is still available to you today. It's called—the power of rejoicing! Anytime you praise God despite your circumstances, the forces of heaven come to your aid.

You say, " But I don't feel like praising God." Then listen, "... offer to God a sacrifice of praise" (Hebrews 13:15 NIV). Anybody can praise Him in the good times, but when you have to rise above your feelings and sacrifice to do it—that's when it's most effective!

The Battle of Jericho teaches us that sometimes we

have to shout when: (1) it makes no sense; (2) it seems like we're just going in circles; (3) the enemy stands over us mocking; (4) our rational mind says "this is no way to win a war;" and (5) it's the last thing on earth we feel like doing.

Nehemiah writes, "... the joy of the Lord [the joy that comes from knowing He is present with you in the situation] is your strength" (Nehemiah 8:10). If you look to your circumstances to find joy, you'll live on an emotional roller coaster. But if you look to the Lord of your circumstances and rejoice in His unchanging goodness, you'll move from weakness to strength every time.

James writes, "Consider it pure joy, my brothers, whenever you face trials ... so that you may be mature" (James 1:2-4 NIV). You see, joy always finds purpose in the pain, advantage in the adversity, and direction in the devastation.

So remember, wherever you go today, God's promise to you is "... ye shall go out with joy ..." (Isaiah 55:12).

Chapter Eleven

Learn to Relax

Some time ago I went to my doctor complaining of chest pain, and he told me that I was under too much stress. He said I was "too intense." That really stressed me, because I thought I'd successfully redirected my intense nature by working intensely for the Lord—kind of like "Super-Christian!"

It took me a long time to learn that no matter how great your cause is, when you push yourself beyond the boundaries of wisdom, you suffer exactly the same results as those who burn out in any other endeavor.

"What can I do?" you ask. Make stress work for you, instead of against you. Here are a few insights to help you:

(1) If you grew up in a stress-filled environment, you may not know how to handle life any other way.

When your only tool is a hammer, you tend to see every problem as a nail! Acknowledge that stress is like emotional adrenaline to you, which is why you keep creating it.

(2) When you're sitting in a chair and you hear the legs crack, the smart money says, "Take your weight off it before you end up on the floor." Heed the telltale signs of stress before your health breaks, and you're no good to God or anybody else.

(3) Learn to be prudent. Listen, "I, wisdom, dwell together with prudence" (Proverbs 8:12 NIV). The word prudence means "careful management." Learn to become a better manager of your time, your energy, and your gifts.

(4) Recognize your "stressors." Simply stated— learn to adapt to change instead of allowing things to pressure you. As long as you think things must always be a certain way, you'll live in frustration, for life has a middle name and it's called "change."

This may come as a revelation to you, but you're supposed to get tired! Fatigue is a God-given boundary that prevents you from pushing yourself over the edge. What is it that gives you acid in your stomach, knots in your neck, and makes you "less than a joy" to be around? Here are three leading contenders:

(a) Imagination. Like virtual reality, it'll cause you to have arguments in your head with people who aren't even around to hear them. Ever do that?

(b) Memory. It'll keep you stuck in the past.

(c) Impatience. Do slow-moving people tick you off? How about slow traffic? Or slow service in a restaurant? Or a slow checker at the supermarket, whose register happens to runs out of tape just as you reach her, or she can't find the price for several of your grocery items?

Jesus said, "Stop allowing yourself to be agitated" (John 14:27 AMP).

You're doing it to yourself! Your unwillingness to accept life as it is will only keep your blood pressure high and your contentment level low. Listen, "In the world you will have frustration ... but be of good cheer ... I have deprived it of its power to harm you" (John 16:33 NLT). Did you get that? The One who dwells within you has deprived the world of its power to harm you. So relax and learn to enjoy yourself more.

Isn't it strange that people who are capable of managing big companies and developing complex budgets don't have the sense to know when they need a break or how to manage their own resources without depleting them?

If you're wise, you won't just put appointments on your calendar, you'll schedule rest periods too. Timely rest restores your energies and maintains your abilities, so that you can function at full capacity. On the other hand, being pulled in too many directions drains your joy and causes you to give less than your best.

Why do we run ourselves into the ground anyway? Are we not aware of our soul's need for rest or the telltale signs of burnout?

We're like the driver who's so concerned about where he's going and how fast he can get there that he doesn't notice that the engine's knocking, the tires are losing air, and the gas tank's almost empty. Then, when the car breaks down, he wonders what happened. The answer is, that he should have heeded the signs—and so should you!

Jesus said, "Are you tired? Worn out? Come to Me. Get away with Me, and you will recover your life ... walk with Me and work with Me—watch how I do it. Learn the unforced rhythms of grace. I won't lay anything heavy or ill-fitting on you. Keep company with Me, and you will learn to live" (Matthew 11:28-30 TM).

Are you overextended? If so, Jesus is saying,

"Come to Me." Now, you can go to church and not come to Him; read the Bible and not come to Him; be very religious and not come to Him. Yet He alone is the source of everything you need.

If you're having trouble maintaining the pace, and the strain is showing up in your family, your health, and your attitude, consider these four things:

(1) Take time out when you need it. Refuse to be driven by others. People have a tendency to think they know what's best for you. But they don't! You know when you need time out.

(2) If your loved ones have to choose between having less or having you, they'll always choose you. The trouble is we don't give them that choice. Look out your lifestyle is your children's blueprint. If you neglect them now, don't be surprised when they neglect you later.

(3) Don't use work as a narcotic. Workaholism, like any other addiction, only masks the real problem. There's an emptiness inside you that only God can fill; and He will if you let Him!

(4) Effort without reward destroys motivation. Whether it's yourself, your children, or your employees, everybody needs time to recharge their batteries. If you work hard, play hard.

The truth is, rest time is the best time to assess your life, your dreams, your heartaches, and your faith; it's what allows you to enjoy the journey, not just the destination.

Chapter Twelve

Choosing the Right Relationships

For years, Monterey, California, was a pelican's paradise, filled with fish canneries. (Remember Cannery Row?) The birds loved it because they didn't have to fish for a meal; they just feasted on what was lying around. But as fish became depleted along the coast and canneries began closing down, the pelicans got into trouble.

You see, pelicans are great fishers. They fly in groups over the waves, and when they find fish they dive and scoop them up. But these birds hadn't fished in years, so they'd grown fat and lazy. Now their easy meals were gone, and they were dying off.

After trying different things, environmentalists

finally found a way to keep them from becoming extinct. They imported pelicans from other areas—ones that were used to hunting every day—and integrated them with the local birds. It worked! The newcomers immediately began fishing for food and it wasn't long before the starving pelicans began to do the same.

Are you starving for success? If you are, one of the best ways to get things moving in your life is to get around achievers! Watch how they work.

Read their books, listen to their tapes, and learn how they think. You'll inevitably become like the company you keep.

Over and over again, when I was entering a new season, God would bring just the right person into my life. In each instance they had two things I needed; knowledge and a willingness to share it.

Solomon wrote, "Become wise by walking with the wise" (Proverbs 13:20 TM). Surround yourself with people who compliment you, not duplicate you! If you're led only by those whose insight is no deeper than your own, how far will you get? Jesus said, "When a blind man leads a blind man, they both end up in the ditch" (Matthew 15:14 TM).

Limiting yourself to those who laugh at the same

jokes, vote for the same party, and share the same ideas robs you of personal growth and forces you to live in a secure, but shriveled world. If you're going to progress to the next level, spend time with those who are already there—or who at least know how to get there.

Your development, and in some cases your healing, can take place only when you cross paths with people who stretch you.

"But what if they make fun of me?" you ask. Only the arrogant do that. The wise respond to seekers, for they themselves are seekers. Risk asking! Refuse to remain a prisoner in a world of ignorance.

"But what if I don't measure up?" you ask. If you don't stand near a ruler, you won't know how much you need to grow—or how much you've already grown.

Having less information doesn't make you a lesser person. Life's a school, and every new acquaintance is a teacher. Whatever others know, they haven't always known it. The greatest indictment against not knowing is not learning, so today seize every opportunity to learn! But make sure you pick the right people!

Remember the story of the scorpion and the frog?

One day a scorpion asked a frog to carry him

across the river on his back because he couldn't swim. The frog replied, "But how do I know you won't sting me while we're crossing?" The scorpion replied, "If I do that, we'll both drown!" After thinking about it, the frog told him to hop on.

Halfway across the river the scorpion stung him anyway.

As they were drowning, the frog said to the scorpion, "But you promised you wouldn't. Why did you sting me?" The scorpion replied, "I couldn't help it. It's my nature to sting!"

Learn to recognize toxic relationships and walk away from them before they take you down with them. Become more discerning about the company you keep. Sever the ties that limit you! A toxic relationship is like a leg with gangrene. If you don't amputate it, the infection will spread. Unless you have the courage to cut off what won't heal, you'll end up losing more—much more!

You can't partner successfully with somebody who doesn't share your goals or your intensity. When you feel passionately about something, but the other person feels complacent, it's like trying to dance The Macarena with somebody who only wants to waltz. You picked the wrong dance partner!

Never walk anywhere with anyone who doesn't share your passion for the thing you're supposed to be doing together. Some issues can be corrected through teaching and leadership, but you can't teach somebody to care! And if they don't care, they'll affect your environment, ruin your productivity, and break your rhythm with constant criticism and complaints.

It's a mistake to use optimism or pressure to force people into accepting your goals. Others can't run on your fuel or become what they're not just because you want them to and believe they can. No, they've got to run on their own steam or they'll drain you!

The key to recognizing the right relationships for your life lies in—listening! People know themselves better than you do, and they'll generally tell you who they are before you get involved with them. Maya Angelou says, "When people tell you who they are, believe them the first time!"

But you've got to listen! If you fail to hear their self-assessments or their confessions because you're too busy giving them your positive-thinking, "Oh-no-that-can't-be-true!" speech, you'll miss what you should be hearing. Listen to them! Use the discernment God has given you, and you'll save yourself years and tears of secret disappointment.

Solomon says, "As iron sharpens iron, so one man sharpens another" (Proverbs 27:17 NIV).

How do you handle correction? Do you take offense? Do you interpret it as rejection? Do you get defensive?

All of us need people who'll be honest with us because we're too easily blinded by our own egos. When God confronted Adam, he blamed Eve. Listen, "The woman whom thou gavest to be with me, she gave me of the tree, and I did eat" (Genesis 3:12). On the other hand, when David was confronted by Nathan over his affair with Bathsheba, he acknowledged, "I have sinned …" (2 Samuel 12:13).

When God sends somebody to correct you, it's because He loves you. He only does that to those He values. And if He doesn't, it's because you're not His child. Listen, "If you are not disciplined, then you are illegitimate children and not true sons" (Hebrews 12:8 NIV). Check your credentials!

Again I ask, how do you handle correction? By killing the messenger? By making sure he or she never gets through to you again? By pointing to your accomplishments and saying, "Look what I've accomplished, what have you done?" By giving in to self-pity and saying, "People just don't understand or appreciate me?"

Peter needed to be corrected by Paul. Joshua needed to be instructed by Moses. In fact, anybody who ever made a difference learned by taking advice.

The Bible says, "If the ax is dull, and its edge unsharpened, more strength is needed but skill will bring success" (Ecclesiastes 10:10 NIV). Your mind needs to be sharpened every day, so stay open to those whom God sends to do it.

Learn to be accountable! Open your life to a few, carefully selected and trusted friends who'll tell you the truth; friends who've earned the right to examine you, question you, and to counsel you. Solomon says, "Wounds from a friend are better than kisses from an enemy!" (Proverbs 27:6). Think about that!

Accountable people usually exhibit four qualities. Check and see if you've got them: (a) Vulnerability—they're capable of knowing when they're wrong and admitting it, even before they're confronted. (b) Teachability—they're willing to hear, quick to learn, and open to counsel. (c) Availability—they're accessible; you can always reach them. (d) Honesty—they hate anything phony and are committed to the truth, regardless of how much it hurts.

You say, "That's a high standard." You're right!

It's a standard that pride can't handle and fragile egos won't tolerate. There's something in each of us that would rather look good than be good!

Don't misunderstand; I'm not suggesting that just anybody should have access to your life. No, that's dangerous. I said, a few carefully selected and trusted friends; ones who've earned the right to come alongside, and when it's appropriate, ask the hard questions, bring perspective, and keep you on track.

When God sends people like that into your life, thank Him for them. Here are four principles that will help you deal with them correctly:

(1) Show appreciation. If somebody has blessed and enhanced you, always acknowledge it. An attitude of "I don't expect it, so I don't give it," will close doors to your future. Never take others for granted and never forget to say, "Thank you."

(2) Carry your own weight. Avoid doing things that can be construed as opportunistic. Look for ways to make your presence an asset and not a liability. Life owes you nothing except an opportunity to grow.

(3) Be open and direct about what you want. Rambling speeches and ulterior motives imply that the other person is some how less intelligent than you—and that can be fatal!

(4) Understand the boundaries. Just because others know somebody well enough to call him by his first name doesn't mean that you should. Err on the side of the formal, not the familiar. If someone says, "Hello, my name is Charles," don't reply with, "What's up, Charlie!" Show respect; don't try to change protocol to suit the environment you're used to. Observe boundaries.

Respect others, and you'll always have people in your life who can help you to get where you need to go.

Chapter Thirteen

Setting Goals

Can you imagine Sir Edmund Hillary being asked how he conquered Mount Everest and answering, "Well, my wife and I just went for a walk one afternoon, and before we knew it we were at the top of the mountain"? You know better!

First, he studied the mountain. Then he developed a plan to climb it. Then he recruited expert guides. Then he established a daily schedule. Then he made sure he had adequate supplies. Then he developed a budget. And most importantly—he understood that it would take perseverance to reach the top.

In his great book, Dare to Succeed, Van Crouch says he came home from work one night, and his dad asked him, "What have you been doing all day?" He replied, "Nothing much." His dad asked, "Then how did you know when you were finished?" Good point! Without goals, how can you measure your progress?

When God gives you a goal, He'll supply all that's required to reach it. Nehemiah wrote, "By day the pillar of cloud did not cease to guide them on their path, nor the pillar of fire by night to shine on the way they were to take. You gave your good Spirit to instruct them. You did not withhold manna from their mouths, and you gave them water for their thirst. For forty years you sustained them in the desert; they lacked nothing" (Nehemiah 9:19-21 NIV).

If you stopped a hundred people and asked them what they were doing to guarantee success in their future and tracked them until they were sixty-five, you would find that: (a) one was wealthy; (b) five were financially secure; and (c) the remaining ninety-four lived and died as dependents.

Did they plan to fail? No, they just failed to plan!

Unless you have a vision for your future, line up your priorities accordingly, set high standards for yourself, and keep your goals before you at all times—you're destined to be one of the ninety-four. Without achievable goals and deadlines, how can you tell how far you've come? Goals are measurable. You can't manage what you can't measure.

Furthermore, if your goals don't demand growth, you should already have reached them; otherwise what's your reason for getting out of bed in the morning?

Unless you determine where you're going, you'll either end up somewhere else or others will determine it for you. The poorest man is not the one without money—but the one without goals. If you want to develop goals for your life, my friend Van Crouch offers the following steps:

(1) Be specific! What do you want to achieve in the next six to twelve months? Break it down into small, manageable pieces. Rome wasn't built in a day, so don't try to change your whole life overnight.

(2) Develop a written plan! Save the hymn, "In the Sweet By-and-By," for another day. Your goals must be specific and have achievable deadlines; otherwise you'll become discouraged.

(3) Get excited about what God has called you to do! Listen, "I press toward the mark for the prize of the high calling" (Philippians 3:14). Get excited about your own "high calling" and press toward it every day.

(4) Develop an unshakable confidence in God!

Find Scriptures that strengthen you in your purpose and stand on them—Scriptures like, "I am the Lord your God who teaches you what is best for you, who directs you in the way you should go" (Isaiah 48:17 NIV).

(5) Follow through regardless! Utilize concentrated energy, controlled attention, and sustained effort.

(6) Establish an "acceptable minimum!" Say to yourself, "This is the very least I'll accept in this specific time frame. Create a written master checklist.

People who break records are people who keep records. Select two or three items from your list daily, write them down, do them, and check them off each night.

If you do these things, you'll never lack motivation!

Mike Murdock says, "The way to kill a man with a great dream is to give him another one." He's right. When you're spread too thin, you risk becoming mediocre at everything and excellent at nothing. Paul the Apostle wrote, "I am bringing all my energies to bear on this one thing ..." (Philippians 3:13 LB). Most endeavors fail for one reason—a broken focus. One of the enemy's favorite tricks is getting you to say yes to too many things.

Because something is good doesn't necessarily

mean it's right for you. When your plate is full doing what God has given you to do, learn to say no to everything else. "No" is an anointed word. It can set you free from other people's expectations or a need for their approval. Furthermore, "No" doesn't mean never; it just means not now.

If you try to fight on every front, you'll wear yourself out and be effective on none. Fighting a battle without spoils is like pouring water on a burning shack. Unless someone's life is in danger, it's not worth saving. Conserve your strength for when it's your home or you've something really important at stake.

You always lose when you: (a) fight the wrong battle; (b) fight at the wrong time; (c) fight when you've no personal stake in it; (d) fight because you constantly need to win in order to feel good about yourself; or (e) fight even though the battle's already been lost, but pride won't allow you to swallow it.

Stay focused on your goals. Keep your eyes on the prize that God has set before you. If the enemy can't defeat you, he'll distract you with side issues or disqualify you by getting you to make bad personal choices.

Either way, he wins and you lose!

Chapter Fourteen

Keep Working on Yourself

Paganini was one of the greatest virtuosos of all time. He performed his first concert at eleven. Ultimately, he revolutionized violin technique forever. When he died in 1840, he bequeathed his violin to his birthplace of Genoa on one condition—that nobody play it ever again. The city fathers agreed and put it in on display. But wooden instruments have a certain peculiarity. So long as they're played, they show no wear. But if they lie unused, they begin to decay, which is what happened to Paganini's violin. Other instruments of the same vintage, handed down from one musician to another, continue to bless the world. But, tragically, Paganini's became a crumbling relic of what it might have been. What a lesson!

Paul told his spiritual son, Timothy, "Do not neglect the spiritual gift you have received" (1 Timothy 4:14 NLT).

Success is a continuing thing. It involves growth and development. It's achieving one thing, then using that as a stepping-stone to something else. There is no stopping place.

Success happens a-day-at-a-time. Every day that you live, you're in the process of becoming. What you ultimately become depends on what you give yourself to. If you want to succeed, take a moment to consider these seven steps carefully.

(1) Make a commitment to grow daily, and it won't be long before you begin to see real change. The poet, Robert Browning, said, "Why stay on earth, except to grow?"

(2) Value the process more than the product. Certain events may be helpful in making your decision, but it's the process that matures you into what God wants you to be.

(3) Don't wait for inspiration. Sometimes you can run on excitement, but most times only discipline will carry you through.

(4) If you pay now, you'll enjoy greater rewards later; and those rewards always taste sweeter.

(5) Dream big! By thinking of limitations, you create them. But when you pursue your dreams, you can go beyond them. Why? Because the God-given potential within you is limitless!

(6) Life is filled with critical moments when you trade one thing for another. Always trade up, not down!

(7) Learn to master your time or you'll never succeed. Henry Kaiser said, "A minute spent in planning, will save you two in execution." Since you can never recover lost time, make every moment count.

The secret of your success is found in your daily routine. Examine yours today. What ruts do you need to get out of? Remember, a rut is simply a grave with the ends kicked out! What habits are consuming your time?

"What difference does a few minutes make?" you ask. You'd be surprised! If you were to save five minutes each day by streamlining your morning routine (taking less time to dress, shave, apply makeup, drink coffee, read the paper, etc.), ten minutes by eliminating the things you do to keep from starting your day, five additional minutes by avoiding idle talkers and other distractions, and ten more minutes by taking a shorter lunch break—you'd gain an additional 125 hours a year. That's three forty-hour workweeks to use for anything you want!

You can double that to six forty-hour workweeks just by watching thirty minutes less of television every day.

Did you hear about the man in the woods who came across a young lumberjack working feverishly to cut down a tree? "What are you doing?" he asked. "I'm sawing down this tree," he replied. The old-timer said, "You look exhausted, how long have you been at it?" The young lumberjack replied, "Over five hours, and I'm beat." Not yet ready to reveal that he himself had spent thirty years as a lumberjack, the older man said, "It looks as if your saw might be a bit dull." "It probably is," said the younger man, "I've been sawing all day." "Then why don't you take a break and sharpen it?" the older man suggested. "The job will go a lot faster if you do."

The young lumberjack replied, "I don't like sharpening, and anyway, I don't have time right now, I'm too busy sawing!"

It's one thing to work hard and another to work smart. Don't just saw—take the time to sharpen. Every five years knowledge in most major fields doubles. That means if you don't stay sharp, you'll be left behind. The opportunities will go to others, and you'll only be qualified to live in a world that no longer exists.

Recently, I read about a man who was upset because he didn't get a promotion he expected. He complained to his boss, "It's not fair—I've had twenty-five years experience." His boss replied, "No, John, you've had one year's experience—over and over again for the last twenty-five years!"

Repeating the same lessons over and over again means you're not learning enough. You need to reach beyond yourself. Study those who've succeeded where you want to succeed in order to know what to do—and what not to do.

Admiral Hyman Rickover said, "Learn from the mistakes of others; you'll never live long enough to make them all yourself." Ben Feldman said, "Only a fool learns from his own experience." When God gives you an opportunity to climb the next rung of the ladder, use these guidelines:

(a) Don't shrink away from people whose experience and expertise are greater than your own. Diversity threatens only the narrow-minded. Paul says, "The sun has one kind of splendor, the moon another and the stars another … " (1 Corinthians 15:41 NIV). We all struggle with insecurity in certain areas; be careful lest yours is misinterpreted as arrogance.

(b) Don't try to impress people by seeking to be their intellectual equal. If you find yourself in a discussion that intimidates you, listen carefully, ask questions, talk only about what you know, and listen attentively to what you don't. The next time you meet, you'll be that much further ahead.

(c) Don't come to class unless you've done your homework. When God starts taking you higher, prepare your speech, your wardrobe, and your mind. Consult a trusted friend who understands where you are and where you're going. If you can't find one, read up until you grasp the basics. Use what you know to help you understand what you don't. Everything you'll ever learn is related to something you already know. Listen, "… precept must be upon precept" (Isaiah 28:10).

Solomon says, "A king rejoices in servants who know what they're doing" (Proverbs 14:35 NLT). The more you prepare yourself, the more opportunities God will give you.

Chapter Fifteen

Live for Others

In our quest for success, Jesus gives us a new measuring rod. Listen, "Normally the master sits at the table and is served … but not here, for I am your servant" (Luke 22:27 NLT).

In Jesus' time foot-washing was reserved not just for servants, but for the lowest of them. Every hierarchy had its "pecking order," and household workers were no exception. The servant on the bottom was expected to be the one on his knees with the towel and the basin.

What a sight! Here the one with the towel and the basin—is Jesus. Think; the hands that shaped the stars now wash away filth. The fingers that formed the mountains now wipe the feet of crude Galilean fishermen.

Hours before His death, His concern is singular—to let His disciples know that in His kingdom, the way up is down; the way to the top is not through intelligence or manipulation, but through humility and service to others.

David wrote, "Blessed is he that considereth the poor; the Lord will deliver him in the time of trouble" (Psalms 41:1).

This verse was one of my mother's favorites. She lived it. Widowed at barely forty and raising three children on a small pension, we didn't have much to spare.

My sister Ruth recalls, "It didn't matter how little we had, I'd find an extra soda bread baking on the old iron griddle, and she'd always manage to come up with an extra bowl of stew for a neighbor who had even less than we did. It was my job to deliver the bread or just a couple of hot boiled potatoes wrapped in a dish towel to some family where the father was out of work, or the mother was sick, or the children were home alone because the parents were out drinking. Years later, I realized what great lessons I was learning then. Mum really understood this verse. She knew if she fulfilled her end of the bargain, God would fulfill His."

In this verse, the word consideration doesn't mean merely "thinking about" something. No, it means much more. The dictionary defines it this way: "something of value, given in order to make a contract binding." That puts teeth into the agreement! It assures us if we do our part, when we're in trouble, God will be there for us.

God told Abraham, "I will bless thee ... and thou shalt be a blessing" (Genesis 12:2). God blesses you for one reason: so that you can be a blessing to others. If your motive is otherwise, don't expect His help.

Listen to how Jesus explained it. "Love your enemies. Let them bring out the best in you, not the worst. When someone gives you a hard time, respond with the energies of prayer for that person. If someone slaps you in the face, stand there and take it. If someone grabs your shirt, gift wrap your best coat and make a present of it. If someone takes unfair advantage of you, use the occasion to practice the servant life. No more tit-for-tat stuff. Live generously. Here is a simple rule of thumb for behavior. Ask yourself what you'd want people to do for you; then grab the initiative and do it for them ... If you only help those who help you, do you expect a medal? Garden-variety sinners do that. If you only give what you hope to get out of it, do you think that's charity? The stingiest of pawnbrokers does that. I tell you, love your enemies. Help and give without expecting a return. You'll never—I promise—regret it" (Luke 6:27-35 TM).

Did you hear that? Love, expecting nothing in return. Give, even though they'll never say thanks. Forgive, even though they won't forgive you in return. Come early, stay late, and invest everything you've got, even though nobody notices.

Paul refers to this kind of lifestyle as "the high calling" (Philippians 3:14). That's because none of us would ever have set such a high standard.

If you think some people are just naturally more loving than others, think again. Love is a choice—one that costs! You can't love somebody while you're staring into a mirror or give to somebody while you're still clinging to what you've got. Love will cost you your time, your money, and your preoccupation with self.

If you're waiting for the love of God to suddenly envelop you like a cloud and turn you into some sort of floating, divine being who just goes through life doing wonderful loving things for others—forget it! There are no prepackaged saints, no "add-and stir" formula that makes God's love gush forth. To be loving, you've got to nail your world to the Cross and make others your priority.

When Jesus found a woman caught in adultery, He sent her home redeemed and restored. If you're going to be like Him, you've got to find people who are hurting, abused, and even in the wrong, and minister to them until they are healed, restored, and right.

Napoleon conquered the world, yet when he died in exile on the island of St. Helena, he was forsaken by all who knew him best. His wife went back to her father. His best friend deserted him without even saying good-bye. Two of his most trusted marshals openly insulted him, and even the faithful servants, who'd slept outside his bedroom door for years, left. Why? Because he was totally self-centered; the people around him felt used, but never appreciated.

What a lesson—especially for you who think, "I don't need others."

If you reach all your goals, but lose the people who matter most, what have you gained? Wake up! What you deposit into your relationships today is all you'll have to draw on later.

Imagine having a story to tell, but nobody to listen; or something to celebrate, but nobody to celebrate with. And worst of all, your influence ending at the grave, because you failed to share with others the things that God had entrusted to you.

Paul writes, "Remember that the Lord will reward each one of us for the good we do" (Ephesians 6:8 NLT).

One winter night an old couple dashed into the lobby of a small Philadelphia hotel, looking for a room. The clerk said, "I'm sorry, but our rooms are all full." As they started to leave, he asked, "Would you be willing to sleep in my room? It's not a suite, but I think you'll be comfortable there." At first they were reluctant, but the hotel clerk insisted, saying, "Don't worry, I can sleep in the office." So they accepted.

Next morning when it was time to check out, the old gentleman said to the clerk, "Thank you. You deserve to be the manager of the best hotel in the country! Maybe someday I'll build one for you!" The amused clerk smiled and thanked him.

Two years later the clerk received a round-trip ticket to New York City, and a letter from the old couple thanking him again for his kindness. They were inviting him to come and visit them. Although he'd almost forgotten the incident, he decided to take them up on their offer.

When he arrived in the city, they took him to the corner of 34th Street and 5th Avenue, where the elderly gentleman pointed to a magnificent multistory hotel and said, "I just built it, and I want you to manage it." The clerk said, "You must be kidding!" "I can assure you I'm not," he replied.

The old gentleman's name was William Waldorf Astor, the hotel was the original Waldorf-Astoria, and the young clerk who had shown him such kindness, was George C. Bolt—its first manager!

Don't forget to sow another seed of kindness today, for you can never tell what your harvest will be!

Chapter Sixteen

Trust God

One day a man planted a tree and asked God for rain to help it grow. And God sent rain. Next, he prayed for sunshine to help it bloom. And God sent sunshine. Finally, he prayed for frost to strengthen its branches. And God sent that too. But the tree died!

Greatly upset, the man decided to consult a master-gardener. "I ordered all the right things to make it grow. What went wrong?" he asked. The gardener took him aside and showed him his own garden, filled with healthy plants and trees. "When I plant a garden," he said, "I ask God to send whatever He feels it needs; I figure He knows best!"

Are you trying to control what's not yours to control? Are you fretting over circumstances you can't change—and even if you could, you'd probably mess them up?

Today God is saying to you, "Be still, and know that I am God" (Psalms 46:10). The reason He says this to us, is that our activity—when born out of the carnal mind—actually prevents Him from showing Himself strong on our behalf.

Now, that doesn't mean we're to be passive or lazy. It just means we're to do whatever He leads us to do without running ahead of Him in the energy of the flesh! It also means that we're to submit everything to Him first, then slow down and wait! In other words, make sure you have a sense of peace to go along with the plans and ideas you believe He's given you.

Ask Him to reveal to you His will in the matter, then "be still" and acknowledge that He's God, He's in charge, and He knows what He's doing! Learn to trust Him without always demanding to know what He's going to do, when He's going to do it, and how He's going to carry it out.

Stay connected!

Jesus said, "I am the vine, ye are the branches" (John 15:5). Until you really understand those words, you'll keep trying to do things that only He can do—things like blessing yourself, promoting your own ministry, solving your own problems, and answering your own prayers.

Or worse, you try to cover up for Him because you think He's not doing it fast enough, and so you stand there like a substitute teacher, trying to make Him look good through human efforts. Give it up; it can't be done! Jesus said, "I am the vine, ye are the branches ..." All you have to do is stay connected!

King Saul's greatest concern was his standing before the people. David's greatest concern was his standing before God. What a difference. When was the last time you prayed, "Lord, make me better?" Most of the time we pray, "Lord, make me bigger." Listen, if you abide, you'll automatically abound!

You've got to know where your help comes from; otherwise you'll waste your time chasing people who have no more power than you do. Your success is in the vine! Your business is in the vine! You future is in the vine! All you have to do is stay connected!

After they'd fished all night and caught nothing, Jesus said to His disciples, "Launch out into the deep, and let down your nets" (Luke 5:4). The real test of faith comes when: (a) nothing you've tried has worked; and (b) the Lord speaks a word to you that seems to make no sense at all.

Listen to Peter's response, "… nevertheless at thy word I will let down the net" (Luke 5:5). That's it—doubt your doubts, but never doubt God. One word from Him can change everything!

Listen to what happened next, "And when they had this done, they inclosed a great multitude of fishes: and their net brake" (Luke 5:6). There are four lessons here for you today:

(1) He'll involve you in one thing to teach you another. Soon He was going to involve them in an even greater miracle—catching multitudes and bringing them into His kingdom.

(2) He'll use the familiar to do the incredible. In their workplace where nothing special ever happened, He suddenly showed up and changed everything. Look for Him today in the familiar—and the unexpected—places in your life.

(3) He'll move you from the security of the shore to the risks of the deep. Why? Because you've got to experience the great storms in order to enjoy the great catches. No risks, no rewards!

(4) When you obey God—nets break, needs are met, minds are blown, and He is glorified. But

remember, the miracle can't begin until you say, "… nevertheless at thy word I will" (Luke 5:5).

Before we end our journey, let's make one more stop—at The Potter's House.

Listen, "The word which came to Jeremiah from the Lord saying, Arise, and go down to the potter's house, and there I will cause thee to hear my words. Then I went down to the potter's house, and, behold, he wrought a work on the wheels. And the vessel that he made of clay was marred in the hand of the potter: so he made it again another vessel, as seemed good to the potter to make it" (Jeremiah 18:1-4).

Have you been asking, "Why am I going through this? God what are you doing in my life?" You'll find your answers here.

The Master Potter is still in the business of forming and filling us. Knowing that really helps— especially when you're on the wheel, and everything seems to be spinning out of control.

Look under the table and see whose foot is on the wheel! If the enemy had been in control, he'd have thrown you off years ago. But he can't because The Potter is in control of the process; He's monitoring your every move!

He's not intimidated by the clay regardless of

where he found it or how flawed it may be. He knows that all He has to do is touch it, and it will become what He wants. Listen, "… as many as received him, to them gave he power to become the sons of God" (John 1:12). This battle is over what you're becoming! Regardless of what you've been up until now, you have the potential to become "a vessel unto honor" (2 Timothy 2:21).

Notice something else. The Potter never presses down on the clay. He always pulls it up, lifting it higher and higher. How wonderful! Hannah said, "He raises the poor from the dust and … seats them with princes" (1 Samuel 2:8 NIV).

God's still in the business of forming and filling! He formed the sea and filled it with fish. He formed the air and filled it with birds. He formed Adam and filled him with His Spirit (otherwise he'd have been a ceramic). And if you allow Him, He'll form you, fill you, and use you for His glory.

But there's one more thing you need to know.

If the Potter doesn't continually wet the clay, it becomes too hard to work with. Think about that for a moment. When we start getting callous, God turns the wheel faster, touches us in just the right places, and introduces the water. "What does water represent?"

you ask. Two things: (1) His Word. Listen, "Now ye are clean through the word which I have spoken unto you" (John 15:2). (2) His ways. Listen again, "When thou passest through the waters, I will be with thee" (Isaiah 43:2).

God will never allow your relationship with Him to be reduced to a formula. It must be ever-flowing, ever-growing, and ever-changing. He has many ways to bless you, and many stages to take you through, so you must remain pliable.

Jeremiah discovered that even though the vessel was marred, it was still in the Potter's hand. Awesome! God never throws us away; nor is His plan for us thwarted because we have a flaw, or struggle in a certain area.

Understand this: whether you're being lifted from the mud, turned on the wheel, or "made over again," at all times and in every situation—you're always in His hand! That's right! When you are broken and wounded, when others give up on you, when you think you can't take it another day, at your lowest point, you're still in His hand.

And you always will be!

Acknowledgments

Destiny and Deliverance—John Maxwell, Thomas Nelson

Dare to Succeed—Van Crouch, Albury Publishing

God's Inspirational Promise Book—Max Lucado, Countryman

Maximize the Moment—T. D. Jakes, Putnam

How to Succeed at Being Yourself—Joyce Meyer, Harrison House

Three Steps Forward, Two Steps Back—Charles R. Swindoll, Thomas Nelson